How to Set Up a T-Shirt

ISBN-13: 978-1479254026

ISBN-10: 1479254029

Copyright Notice

All Rights Reserved © 2012 Bonney Vallance

This book is a work of the author's experience and opinion. This book is licensed for your personal enjoyment only. This book may not be re-sold or given away to other people. If you would like to share this book with another person please purchase an additional copy for each person you share it with. You may not distribute or sell this book or modify it in any way. The editorial arrangement, analysis, and professional commentary are subject to this copyright notice. No portion of this book may be copied, retransmitted, reposted, downloaded, decompiled, reverse engineered, duplicated, or otherwise used without the express written approval of the author, except by reviewers who may quote brief excerpts in connection with a review. The scanning, uploading and distribution of this book via the internet or via any other means without permission of the publisher is illegal and punishable by law. The publisher does not have any control over and does not assume any responsibility for author or third-party websites or their content. United States laws and regulations are public domain and not subject to copyright. Any unauthorized copying, reproduction, translation, or distribution of any part of this material without permission by the author is prohibited and against the law. Disclaimer and Terms of Use: No information contained in this book should be considered as financial, tax, or legal advice. Your reliance upon information and content obtained by you at or through this publication is solely at your own risk. The authors or publishers assume no liability or responsibility for damage or injury to you, other persons, or property arising from any use of any product, information, idea, or instruction contained in the content or services provided to you through this book. Reliance upon information contained in this material is solely at the reader's own risk. The authors have no financial interest in and receive no compensation from manufacturers of products or websites mentioned in this book. Whilst attempts have been made to verify information provided in this publication, neither the author nor the publisher assumes any responsibilities for errors, omissions or contradictory information contained in this book. The author and publisher make no representation or warranties with respect to the accuracy, applicability, fitness, or completeness of the contents of this book. The information contained in this book is strictly for educational purposes. The author and publisher do not warrant the performance, effectiveness or applicability of any information or sites listed or linked to in this book.

HOW TO SET UP A T-SHIRT BUSINESS

Bonney Vallance

I dedicate this book to everyone who has been lucky enough to start a t-shirt business...

Contents

- Starting Your T-Shirt Business: An Overview
- Naming Your T-Shirt Business
- Drawing Up a Business Plan
- Calculating Your Start-up Costs
- How to Obtain Small Business Grants
- Getting Insurance for Your T-Shirt Business
- How to Trademark Your T-Shirt Business Name and Logo
- Writing an LLC Operating Agreement
- Writing a Company Brochure
- Leasing Office Space
- Managing Your Employees
- How to Market Your T-Shirt Business

Starting a T-Shirt Business:
An Overview

Have you been considering setting up a t-shirt business, but aren't quite sure if it's really the right venture for you?

Many people dream of starting their own business, but hesitate to do so because they have a family to take care of.

So they stay in corporate jobs, sitting at their desks all day, going through piles of documents. They don't necessarily enjoy the work, but they stay with it, thinking there's too much at risk for them to even try opening their own business.

Are you one of these people willing to settle?

Do you want to open your very own t-shirt business?

Are you willing to do what it takes to turn your dream into reality or will you back down at the thought that a t-shirt business requires a lot of hard work and involves too much risk?

Running your very own t-shirt business carries a lot of advantages. Among other things, you get to be your own boss, do things your way, set up your own schedule, and generally take control over your own future.

A t-shirt business also allows you to let your creative juices flow freely.

The good news is that there have been many individuals who have successfully realised their dream of running their own t-shirt business and you, too, can realise that dream.

Of course, you'll need to take a few things into consideration, among which is the task of competing with big brands. You'll be pleased to know that it's now so much easier to take advantage of the common shortcomings of these commercial giants because customers have become significantly savvier.

Your competitive advantage

The biggest advantage of big stores is their ability to offer low prices. However, you can easily negate this advantage by thinking about what your target market wants that they normally can't find in a big t-shirt store.

One of the most effective ways for you to set yourself apart and step way ahead of these large stores is by making sure you have excellent customer service skills.

Plus you can offer a more specialized range of t-shirt—ones that are hard to find in the big faceless commercial stores.

Pretty and profitable?

Aside from being enjoyable and providing you with an outlet for your creativity, a t-shirt business can also be very profitable.

This is, in fact, among the biggest advantages of this business venture and many people have taken advantage of a t-shirt business's potential for earning a great deal of money.

Of course, becoming successful isn't guaranteed in this business – or in any other business, for that matter. But, earning well while having fun is certainly something many people aspire to.

Identify your target market

Before you even open your t-shirt business, you should already have decided what kinds of goods you'll be selling and this decision will depend largely on your target market.

Identifying your target market is perhaps the very first thing you need to do because the kind of products you'll be selling is highly dependent on the type of individuals you'll be selling to.

You can choose to focus on fashion tees, funny tees, tees for skaters, children's or novelty tees, or whatever area of t-shirt culture you're interested in.

Because students are the ones who are typically more interested in t-shirt culture, you may want to focus your t-shirt business on their needs.

You should then do some research to find out what types of t-shirts are currently popular with your identified group.

Remember that the clothing business is a very broad industry and your t-shirt business needs to cover a specific niche in order to ensure success.
Once you've found your niche, you'll need to gain a deeper understanding of that niche and keep up with its trends so you can offer your customers only the best the world of t-shirts has to offer.

Clothes for cash flow

Next up are your cash flow projections. Make sure your projections are as conservative as possible so you'll have a wide margin for error. There are just too many aspiring entrepreneurs who make the mistake of setting their projections so high that they end up with cash flow problems.

Remember that a steady cash flow is essential to making sure your business doesn't become just another failed enterprise. Inaccurate projections are among the major reasons for many businesses failing within the first three years of operations. You need to make sure you don't become part of this statistic.

Towards that end, you should do your books daily or hire a bookkeeper for that purpose. This helps you catch money drains early on and take measures to stop it.

Treat them like kings

Customer service is another important component of running a t-shirt business.

People who buy from niche t-shirt businesses typically do so because of the special treatment and personalized service they get.

Customers naturally love being treated like they're special.

They're looking for personal service, professional and honest advice, and a wealth of information on the products they're interested in. You may even know them by name if they're repeat customers.

This part of the entire t-shirt business experience is one you should never take for granted if you're serious about successfully running your own t-shirt business.

You may start out as a one-man or woman operation, but sooner or later you're going to need help in running your t-shirt business, in which case you need to make sure you hire the right people.

You should also be sure to hire efficient staff with excellent customer service skills before you open your business.

Your employees should be able to assist customers capably and provide expert information about the goods you carry.

Therefore, you'll need to provide your staff with adequate training to make sure they know exactly what they're doing when they deal with your customers. This enhances your chance of succeeding at your business venture.

Bear in mind that a large part of your success will lies on the competence of your staff. A single incompetent employee can, in fact, have a hugely negative impact on the business.

In the same way, competent employees are likely to attract more customers to your business. The friendlier and more approachable your employees are, the likelier it is for customers to come back and even refer your business to their family and friends.

Bear in mind that the t-shirt industry is constantly growing and the number of niche t-shirt companies is exploding.

You can expect competition to be tough, which is why you need to take all the necessary steps to make your business stand out.

Careful planning and close attention to detail should help you accomplish what you set out to do.

Once you have everything set up, you'll need to let your target market know of your existence so you can start building your initial customer base.

You'd do well to develop an advertising and marketing plan that's sure to kick-off your operations. Among your first steps should be making sure your opening day is a grand event.

This is probably your best chance of drawing a lot of attention to your t-shirt business, so be sure to carry it out with a bang!

So now we have covered the overview let's get down to specifics.

Stay at home

You may also have heard some people saying that it's easy to start a t-shirt business right from your own home.

The hard truth is that it's not always easy to start any type of business from home.

This doesn't mean you should just forget about your dream of running your own t-shirt business, of course.

It simply means you need to have the right expectations while your business is still in the planning stage.

Take note that while a t-shirt business may not really pay high wages, it does provide steady employment that can be far more enjoyable than monotonous office work.

If you seriously want to run your own business, then you'll need to develop close attention to detail, which is essential in this business.

You'll need to have adequate mathematical skills as well, so you can keep track of your business' accounting.

In principle, starting a t-shirt business is quite simple, since it's easy enough to understand what needs to be done.

But actually doing what needs to be done may not be as easy as you think. You therefore need to ask yourself if you're really up to the task.

Here are a few questions to consider:

- Do you have the necessary skills for market research?

- Can you put together a simple yet workable business plan?

- Do you have the kind of focus, patience, dedication, and passion necessary to execute your plan?

More importantly, you'll have to ask yourself just how badly you want to have your own business.

Start small

Perhaps you'd like to test the waters first by setting up a small business that you can operate from home.

This way, you get to start your dream business with minimal capital investment and gain the necessary experience that will help prepare you for the big leagues as well.

A big difference

However, you need to realise that it also involves a considerable amount of hard work. You'll need to screen-print your bestsellers every single day; perhaps even two to three times each day, depending on the demand.

Therefore, the very first thing you need to do if you're planning to open your own t-shirt business is to understand and accept the fact that there's a huge difference between commercial t-shirt business and your occasional t-shirt printing spree.

That being said, it can be relatively easy to start your very own home-based t-shirt business.

Learn to screen-print

Most importantly, if you're really serious about starting your own t-shirt business, then you first have to learn how to screen-print.

Enrol in a t-shirt printing course, preferably in a reputable college.

You may have to enrol in several different clothing and printing-related courses, since a single short course that lasts for a few months is likely to offer just a small portion of the knowledge you need to gain in order to successfully operate your own t-shirt business.

If possible, try to enrol in a course combining theoretical learning with practical application.

First step

The first step is to decide on your style of t-shirt and then figure out how much it costs to make it. This means you need to account for every single component, including that little bit of fabric you use for your tags as well as the cost of power utilized.

Next

Your next step will then be to double the cost of the product and then set that as your selling price. Don't be discouraged if one t-shirt turns out to cost more than $20. Take note that people are willing to pay more for a unique product.

Getting buyers

Now it's time to decide to whom you'll be selling your t-shirts.

How do you go about getting your established buyers?

You'll have to do some leg work, of course. Draw up a list of local establishments (local skateboard shops and clothes shops) you'd like to do business with and then bring your samples along.

Visit the business owner when they're not too busy to make sure you get their full attention. Ask to speak with the owner or whoever's in-charge of operations.

Let them sample your wares

Bring samples of your best tees to see if they'd be willing to sell your products. After making your pitch, offer to leave one of your samples with the owner to help him make his decision and don't forget to leave your contact information, of course.

If your products are as good as you think, then you're likely get a call within a few days, possibly for a small first order. Be prepared to keep up with a consistent demand for your products once they've become regular features in your partner establishments.

They're likely to ask if you have all the necessary permits and licenses for your t-shirt business.

Be honest and tell them that's the very first thing you're going to do once you've established that you have enough of a market to make the home business worth your while.

If you already have the appropriate licenses, then you can get right down to business and get real commitments from these business owners to sell your products in their respective establishments.

You'll then need to take into account the number of options available to you for selling your t-shirts.

Things to consider:

- How many skateboard shops or clothing shops are willing to sign a contract confirming that they'll be selling your goods on a regular basis?

- How will each of these establishments pay you for your goods?

- Can you rely on each of them to pay you on time?

Regular customers

Take note that your primary goal in establishing an initial customer base should be to get as many establishments as possible to commit to ordering some of your products on a regular basis.

Once these institutional buyers have been established, you'll be in a much better position to start marketing your products to individual customers who are likely to buy just one t-shirt at a time.

If your t-shirts are as good as your family and friends say they are, then you can expect to get large orders from your institutional buyers. In due time, your products should become a regular feature in their outlets, in which case your biggest problem will probably be that of keeping up with the demand.

Top tip

Another useful tip is to stick to making t-shirts that are proven bestsellers. You may venture into related products in time, but be sure to do it cautiously and only after thorough testing.

When you do start establishing your t-shirt business, make sure you have all the necessary permits and licenses for your business. You also have to make sure that all regulations, storage and parking permits, and building codes are complied with.

Talk to your local authorities

Take note that there are a lot of things you need to take into consideration if you're getting into the clothing business.

Among the things you need to consider are waste chemicals (from printing inks), water and garbage issues, plumbing issues, and fire codes. The best way to address these concerns, of course, is to consult the local authorities.

All above board

Among the things you need to ensure when you start a business is that your operation stays within legal bounds.

Visit your local municipal building to check on the legal requirements for home businesses within your area. If you're lucky, then your locality will be one of those with requirements that are relatively easy to fulfill. Be sure to include these fees in calculating your start-up budget.

The rules and regulations for operating a business from home depends largely on where you live, so you'll need to find out exactly what you need to do to be granted a permit and then make sure you do it. After all, there's no better way to start a business than to make sure it's legit.

Doing everything within legal bounds right from the start is the best way to start any business. Taking shortcuts may just lead to some serious and quite expensive legal problems later on.

So, challenging as it may be, you should do whatever it takes to secure a business license before opening your home-based t-shirt business.

Price

The next thing you need to take care of is your price list. You should therefore set a price structure that allows you to pay yourself a good wage, take care of your taxes (about 25% for self-employed individuals), and still get a net profit that makes the time and energy spent at running the business well worth it.

Hazards

Fire hazards and storage space are also among the things you need to take into consideration when planning your business. And you may not realise this, but powdered ink is considered a combustible item.

For this reason, you'll most probably need to have a separate storage area from your house.

This area should be large enough for all of your components and materials, and it should be designed specifically for purposes of storing your stock.

Among other things, your storage area will need adequate reinforcement on the ceiling as well as on all of its sides. You'd also do well to have a fire door built.

Electrical concerns

For one thing, you'll probably need to hire an electrician to review the electrical connections in your house.

Some printing appliances may even require special grounding specifications and different types of wire code. Even if you don't need to make enhancements in your wiring system, you'll still need to have it checked by a professional to be sure.

Take note as well that the motors that power the equipment commonly used in a t-shirt business use up a lot more energy than your typical household appliances, so you should be prepared for a significant increase in your electricity bills.

Ventilation

When running a t-shirt business, you'll also need to make sure your workroom has enough extraction and ventilation to keep your working area cool.

Find out if your locality demands a high or low working temperature environment. Ventilation and extraction requirements may also depend on the kind of machinery you'll be using in your t-shirt business.

Neighbours

Your neighbours may also complain about the additional traffic causing so much noise and the increase in garbage, which typically has a terrible smell in hot weather and tends to attract vermin of all sorts.

Take note that with neighbours disapproving of your business venture, local authorities aren't likely to grant you the necessary permits and licenses for your t-shirt business. Even if your neighbours don't complain, you may still have to contend with the issue of additional garbage.

You'll likely be required to pay for two or more garbage pick-ups and you'll most probably be required to use a protected container for your business garbage instead of the usual household garbage bin.

Noise

Another thing your neighbours may have cause to complain about is the noise generated by your sewing machinery. They'd most likely love the design of your tees, but definitely not the noise.

Keep things separate

As you start turning your home into a t-shirt business, you need to avoid making the common mistake of combining the materials you use for your personal life with those you use for the t-shirt business.

What you need to do is set up a closet or storage room for your t-shirt inventory and then store the components and materials for home use in a separate closet or cupboard. Once all these are properly set up, you can start fulfilling orders.

It's t-shirt time!

Naming Your T-Shirt Business

Choosing a company name can be the most fun part of starting a company. It can also be one of the most important.

After all, having the right t-shirt business name can be a very effective advertising tool. Among other things, it can give prospective customers a general idea of what your company does and what you have to offer. In the same way, choosing the wrong name is likely to drive would-be customers away.

Here are a couple of things to remember when choosing a business name:

Keep it short and memorable

Needless to say, a short company name is much easier to remember than a lengthy one. Choosing a short name doesn't just involve using less words, but also words with less syllables. But, aside from being short, your business name also has to be catchy so as to promote better name recall.

You are your name

This means your company name should reflect the company's personality.

It should give people a general idea of what services you provide or what benefits they can get from patronizing your business.

You need to have an image which you want your t-shirt business to project and the name you choose must fit that image.

More importantly, you have to choose a name your target customers can easily connect with.

Now, you know the basics of choosing a company name and you realize how important a name is to your business.

However, you shouldn't take the process of choosing a name too seriously.

While the company name does have to reflect its personality, it doesn't really have to define your company completely. Take note that venturing into other related businesses is a normal part of any company's growth, so there is a real possibility that you may have to change your business name from time to time.

Again, the name of your business is important, but you shouldn't get hung up on the process of choosing it.

As long as you make sure that it's memorable, it tells people what your business is about, and you're proud of it, then you're good to go.

Drawing Up a Business Plan

Developing a new business naturally requires a good foundation, and building such a foundation begins with having a sound business plan.

Remember that the business plan is an essential part of documenting a start-up business' financial goals, business objectives, and marketing plans.

Implementation of all your t-shirt business ideas can only successfully begin once you've completed your business plan.

Choosing the Right Format

You probably already know that a business plan ranks among the most vital components of starting your t-shirt business and ensuring its success.

But, how exactly do you make a good business plan?

Well, there are several variations and templates you can choose from. What's important is for you to choose the one that's best suited to the kind of enterprise you'll be running and to the purpose for which you're making the plan in the first place.

Here are some of the things you need to take into consideration:

1. Your Target Audience

There are two types of business plan.

a. There are business plans intended for an internal audience and these plans are usually part of your t-shirt business growth strategy; they're also usually referred to as strategic plans.

b. There are also plans meant for external audiences and the purpose of these plans is usually to attract financing, suppliers, or talent for your t-shirt business.

If the purpose of your business plan is primarily to get funding, then the document will typically be in condensed form, or a sort of summary of a more comprehensive business plan.

Such a version is generally known as a *funding proposal* or a *business opportunity document* and it's usually followed by the larger plan.

A business plan can indeed be a very useful document, so it's important to clearly define the audience for which it is intended.

2. What Goes Into the Plan?

Remember that a business plan needs to be comprehensive and that it's essentially created to put into writing what you envision for your t-shirt business venture.

Your t-shirt business plan should contain:

- An executive summary
- The background and history of your company
- A clear description of your t-shirt business concept
- Your marketing analysis and development plan
- Your operations and production assessment
- Your financial assessments and projections
- Your human resources management assessment and plan
- Your business implementation plan
- An identification of resources
- The proposed investor deal structures wherever appropriate
- A survival strategy that describes potential risks and mitigation measures
- Your t-shirt business growth strategy

- Your exit strategy
- Appendices

If that seems daunting, don't worry. Some of the components of your business plan may be longer than others and some of them are optional, depending on your target audience, the format you choose to adopt, and the purpose of your plan.

What's important is for your intended reader to clearly grasp the value proposition, understand why your t-shirt business is expected to succeed, and how that success will be achieved.

If you're pitching the plan to potential investors, (or most probably the bank) then they should quickly understand your proposed deal structure and the possible returns.

3. What Length To Make Your Plan

The average business plan typically consists of 20 pages, though there are some that contain a hundred pages or more. The length of your plan will depend largely on its purpose and your target audience.

If the primary purpose of your business plan is to attract investors, then you can expect it to contain more details and therefore be lengthier than a plan that's primarily for communicating your t-shirt business growth strategy.

In the same way, the business plan for a venture with a relatively simple concept should be a lot more concise than one that's made for a highly complicated enterprise.

4. Should You Use a Template or Pay a Consultant?

Many people are also confused as to whether they should hire a consultant to help them write their business plan or simply use a template for guidance.

Well, it can be quite tempting to use a template or get someone else to make the plan for you. However, it's still best if you write the plan yourself even if you do decide to get some guidance from a consultant.

After all, who knows your business better than you?

A solid business plan is perhaps the easiest way for you to communicate your t-shirt business ideas to your target audience as well as to help you prevent problems and identify business growth strategies.

It can also be your most valuable tool when you're in search of funding for your t-shirt business.

Remember, though, that instead of treating it as a blueprint or a strict manual which you should implement to the letter, the plan should be seen as more of a guide in operating your t-shirt business.

TIP: Even if you don't have an immediate audience for your plan, the document and even the process itself will definitely prove to be of value to your business in the long run.

Preparing a solid business plan for all the right reasons can indeed increase your chances of attaining success in your t-shirt business.

How to Write the Executive Summary

The executive summary generally serves as the introduction to your formal and comprehensive business plan.

You could even say that this is Part 1 of your business plan.

It contains a summary of your t-shirt business proposition, present business status, financial projections, and the key elements for success.

Although it's often tempting to just rush through this component of your business plan, always remember that an executive summary is likely to be the very first thing your target investors or banking officials will read in the document.

It basically tells the reader the status of the company currently, and where it's expected to go. Many people aren't likely to read the remainder of the plan if the executive summary doesn't catch their interest, so it's really very important to do this right.

The importance of the executive summary lies in the fact that it tells your reader exactly why you believe your t-shirt business will be a success.

Brevity is the key to a solid executive summary, which generally ranges from half a page to a maximum of two pages.

Writing anything longer puts you at risk of losing the reader's attention and appearing unfocused. If you can keep the summary under one page without sacrificing quality, then do so.

Note: Although it serves as the introduction, it's best to write the executive summary after you've completed your business plan. After all, it is basically a shorter version of your plan.

To keep the summary consistent with the plan itself, it should have the following components:

1. Your Mission Statement

Your business plan's executive summary is be the best place for you to express your mission statement. Make sure that statement is concise and explains in as few words as possible the existence of your t-shirt business, its goals, and how you plan to achieve those goals.

In short, it should explain your t-shirt business thrust to the reader. Remember to keep your mission statement focused and direct, leaving no room for confusion as regards what your t-shirt business venture is all about.

2. What's Your Business Concept?

In describing your t-shirt business concept, you'll need to offer some details about the kind of t-shirt business you'll be running, who your target customers are, and what your competitive advantages are.

You may point out that you're filling a void you've identified in the market, offering better prices for comparable services in the industry, or offering a better service than what's currently available.

3. A Little Background

You may also want to give your reader an idea of when your venture began, who the founders are and what functions they perform, how many employees you have (or plan to hire), and where the t-shirt business is located and if there are any subsidiaries or branches.

A description of your offices and facilities as well as the services your offer would also be a good idea.

4. Your T-shirt business Status and Financial Outlook

You'll also need to give a short description of the current status of your t-shirt business.

Explain if your business is still in the conceptualization stage, if you've already started setting it up, or if it's already fully operational and you're simply planning to expand.

You should also mention your expected costs and your financial projections for both the short term and the long term.

This will give potential investors an idea of how much capital you need and if your business venture matches the kind of opportunity they're currently looking for.

If you already have existing investors, then you'd do well to provide some information on them as well.

5. Key Factors for Success

The reader of your business plan will also appreciate getting a preview of the key factors for t-shirt business success.

These factors depend on your situation, of course, but it generally includes technology patents, strategic partnerships, market factors and economic trends.

If your t-shirt business is already fully operational and you've had some successful projects worth noting (you may have been the first to offer a certain service in the industry), then you should include that as well.

Finally...

All in all, your business plan's executive summary should provide its reader with a quick but insightful glimpse into the plan itself.

It's advisable to highlight everything except the mission statement in bulleted lists. Include all of the important points without revealing too much, since each section is discussed in detail within the plan itself, anyway.

More importantly, make sure the summary sells the proposal on its own as much as possible, just in case reader doesn't read your plan. It does happen!

Note: It's also a good idea to draw up a table of contents right after the executive summary so the reader will know where he can find each section in the plan itself.

If you're still in the process of setting up your t-shirt business, then you likely won't have much to write as regards to some of the areas listed above. In that case, focus on your own experience and expertise in the field, and the circumstances that led to your t-shirt business concept. Tell your target readers how you plan to set your t-shirt business apart from the competition and convince them that there's indeed a need for your business within your target niche or industry.

Company History

After the executive summary, your business plan should contain a section covering your business background or company history.

The length of this portion and how it's told will depend largely on how far along your t-shirt business is in terms of operations and development.

Naturally, the business history of a venture that's just starting is totally different from one that's been operating for some time. It should be about one page long, though it's understandable for a start-up company's history to cover less than an entire page.

What to Include

In this section, you should be able to illustrate how the various elements of your t-shirt business venture fit together and form one successful enterprise.

You should also include some background information on the nature of the t-shirt business itself and identify the factors that are expected to facilitate its success.

Furthermore, don't forget to mention the specific market needs you're planning to satisfy and the ways and methods in which you expect to satisfy these needs.

If possible, you should also identify the specific individuals or groups of people whom you believe have those needs.

An example of a specific market could be:

Men and women aged 18 to 30 with an income of $40,000 within 50 miles of your location.

How It All Started

Among the things you should include in the company history portion of your business plan is the origin of your t-shirt business concept.

This explains how you first came upon the idea for your t-shirt business and why you decided to pursue that idea. You should also indicate the progress you've made so far as regards operating and growing your business venture. If you're still in the process of starting your business, then say so.

NOTE: It's also a good idea to mention the problems you've encountered along the way and how you handled each of them.

Potential investors and business partners will surely appreciate knowing that they're dealing with someone who's not afraid to deal with challenges from time to time.

Projected Short-Term Growth

You would also do well to include your short-term business growth plans in this section, so the reader will know that you've thought about your venture carefully and that you have concrete plans for its growth.

NOTE: If you're just starting a new t-shirt business, then you may want to include a bit of personal history along with your background.

Among the things you can include are your educational history, technical skills, areas of expertise, relevant professional club memberships, and other t-shirt businesses you may have started or companies you worked for.

TIP: You may even want to share your areas of inexperience or weaknesses and how you intend to compensate for these areas.

Your target investors would definitely appreciate knowing that you're aware of the things you need to improve on and are making concrete efforts at improving them.

Finally...

In summary, the company history section of your business plan should provide an interested reader with a much better idea of how your t-shirt business came to be and who you are as a businessperson. Again, the key is to keep this section concise and avoiding unwanted information.

Organization and Management

This section of your plan includes the following:

- Your company's organizational structure
- The profiles of your management team
- Details about company ownership
- The board of director's qualifications

It's important for you to answer the question of who does what when you prepare this section.

Explain what each person's background and qualifications are. Tell your reader exactly why you've brought or are bringing these people into your organization and management team.

What exactly are they responsible and accountable for?

NOTE: You may think this section of the plan is unnecessary if you're setting up a small venture with less than five people on your team, but anybody reading your business plan needs to know who's in charge.

Therefore, you should still provide a description of every department or division, along with their functions, regardless of the size of your company.

If there's an advisory board for your business, then you should also identify who's on it and how you plan to keep each member on the board.

- What salary and benefits do you plan to provide for members of your team?

- Will you be offering incentives? If so, what are they?

- How do you plan to handle promotions?

In this section of your business plan, you need to reassure your audience that the people on your team aren't going to be just names on your company letterhead.

What's Your Structure?

One very simple yet effective way of presenting your organizational structure is by creating an organizational chart and then providing a narrative description of the chart.

By doing this, you don't leave anything to chance, you're making sure the functions and responsibilities of each team member has been carefully thought out, and you've ensured that someone's in charge of each and every function in your t-shirt business. Therefore, no function is taken for granted and there'll be no overlapping of responsibilities.

TIP: Remember that this kind of assurance is very important to your reader, especially if that reader is a potential investor.

Management Profiles

Ask any business expert and he'll probably tell you that among the most significant success factors in any business is the track record and ability of the management team.

This is why it's important for you to provide your reader with a background of the key members of the management team. (Don't worry if your just starting out. You won't have management staff at this stage).

Specifically, you'd do well to provide resumes that indicate the name, position and the corresponding functions, primary responsibilities and level of authority, educational background, skills and experience, number of years on your team (unless it's a start-up company), compensation level and basis, previous employment and track record, industry recognitions received, and community involvement.

TIP: When you indicate the track record of your team, be sure to quantify their achievements.

For example, instead of saying:

"Extensive experience in managing a sales department"

you could say:

"Successfully managed a sales department of ten people for 15 years."

It's also a good idea to highlight how the key members of the management team complement your own experience and expertise.

If you're starting a new t-shirt business, then show your reader how the unique experiences of each member of your team can contribute to your business venture's overall success.

Company Ownership

Aside from the organizational structure, this section of the plan should also describe the legal structure and provide important ownership information regarding your t-shirt business.

- Has the business been incorporated? If so, then is it an S or a C corporation?

- Is your business a partnership?

- If so, then is it a limited or general partnership?

- Or are you the sole proprietor of your t-shirt business?

The most important pieces of information you should include in this section are the owner/s' names, ownership percentage, form of ownership, degree of involvement of each owner within the business, common stock, and outstanding equity equivalents.

Board Qualifications

Take note that there's a huge advantage to setting up an unpaid board of advisors for your company, as it can provide you with the kind of expertise the company is otherwise unable to afford.

Simply by enlisting the help of some successful businessmen who are popular in the industry and including them in your advisory board, you'll definitely go far in enhancing the credibility of your company and encouraging a perception of expertise.

If the company has a board of directors, then you need to provide the names of the board members, their respective positions in the BOD, their background, the extent of their involvement with the t-shirt business, and their expected contribution to its success.

Market Analysis

You may be a hundred percent confident about the quality of the service your t-shirt business has to offer, but unless you're able to connect with your target customers, quality won't do you much good.

You'll have to get your service into your customers' hands, so to speak, to get the necessary sales.

And that's why you need market analysis. This section of your business plan should be used to illustrate your knowledge of the industry. You may also use it to present highlights and conclusions from the marketing research data you've collected.

For your analysis to be reliable, you need to study the three Cs of marketing:

1. Company
2. Customer
3. Competition

Of course, it's understandable that you should be aware of your company's strengths and weaknesses, but you should also know the same things about your competitors so you'll get a better idea of how to deal with them.

More importantly, you need to know who your customers are and what their needs and wants really are.

When you prepare the company analysis component of this section, you'll need to describe the primary industry to which your business belongs, the industry's current size and historic growth rate, the industry's characteristics and trends, and the industry's major customer groups.

All these will put into perspective the description you'll provide of the company you've established or are planning to establish.

Who Are Your Target Customers?

In choosing and defining your target customers, make sure that you narrow it down to a size that you're sure you can manage.

Many business owners make the mistake of trying to provide everything to everybody at once. Slow and sure is often a better philosophy where your business is concerned.

This section of your plan should include information that identifies the unique characteristics of your target customers including:

- Their needs
- The extent to which these needs are being met
- Demographics.

It's also a good idea to identify your target market's geographic location, who among them makes the major decisions, and any market trends that may affect your business.

The size of your target market should also be indicated in this section, along with your expected market share gains and the reason for these expected gains.

You should also indicate your pricing schedule as well as your gross margin targets and whatever discount structures you may be planning.

You'd also do well to identify what resources you plan to use to get information as regards your target market, the media you'll be using to reach the market, your target market's purchasing cycle, and the socio-economic trends likely to affect your target market.

If all this sounds complicated don't worry, just break down each section and do it one at a time.

Your Competition

Of all the Cs you need to study, your competition may be the toughest, especially if you're new to the industry. The first thing you need to do is study your direct competitors.

If you're planning to operate a t-shirt business in your district, then you're likely to get direct competition from the likes of the larger multinational t-shirt businesses. So it pays to examine all the possible options on how you can set your t-shirt business apart.

It's important for you to identify your direct competitors according to product or service line and market segment.

You should then assess their weaknesses and strengths, determine the level of importance of your own target market to your competitors, and identify the barriers that may pose a challenge as you enter your target niche.

This may include high investment costs, changing technology, existing patents or trademarks, customer resistance, and a difficulty in finding quality personnel.

You'd also do well to determine the market share of each key competitor and then provide an estimate of the time it'll take for new competitors to enter the niche.

Aside from looking for ways to set yourself apart from the competition, you'll also want to see how your business fits into the marketplace itself. In doing so, you'll have to consider the strengths and weaknesses of your competitors, the possibility of competitors leaving the marketplace and new ones entering it, the services your competitors are relying on for a majority of their revenue, and effective ways of overcoming possible threats from substitute services.

Developing Your Marketing Strategy

Once all three Cs have been addressed, you should be ready to start developing your marketing program.

This basically involves an analysis of what's known as the "four Ps."
They are:

1. Product,

2. Place,

3. Price,

4. Promotion.

Product, of course, refers to what you plan to sell (in this case your t-shirt business service) Place refers to where you plan to sell it (office, online, or both).

Price refers to the amount you'll charge for each service you'll be offering.

And Promotion refers to the incentives and other promotional strategies you plan to use in order to get your target market to try your services.

To put it simply, a marketing strategy is your way of drawing in customers, which is indeed very important since customers are essentially the lifeblood of any business venture.

There isn't a single way of approaching a marketing strategy. What's important is for your strategy to be uniquely applicable to your t-shirt business and part of a continuing evaluation process that aims to facilitate business growth and success.

In conducting a "four Ps" analysis, you'll likely conduct some market tests and you'd do well to include the results of these tests in this section of your business plan.

All other details of the tests may be attached as an appendix.

The information you provide in this section may include the number of customers who participated in the tests, demonstrations or any information provided to the participating customers, the degree of importance of satisfying the needs of your target market, and the percentage of participants who expressed desire to take advantage of your products and/or services.

After creating your marketing strategy, you'll also need to draw up a sales strategy, which outlines the methods you'll be using to actually sell the services you plan to offer.

There are two very important elements of a good sales strategy.

- The first is your sales force strategy, which determines if you'll be employing internal sales personnel or independent representatives. You should also identify the number of people you plan to recruit for your company's sales force as well as the recruitment and training strategies you'll be using.

You'd also do well to present the compensation packages you've lined up for your sales personnel.

- The second element of a sales strategy is a description of the sales activities you've lined up for the company. A sales strategy is made more manageable when broken down into activities.

For example, you could start with identifying prospective customers and then prioritizing your prospects according to those who have the highest potential of buying your products.

From this outline of activities, you can easily determine the number of prospects you may have to get to make a sale and the average amount you'll likely earn from each sale.

You'll also need to draw up a solid market development plan in order to make your market analysis work to your advantage.

While the information in your development plan is likely to come into play only when your company has been established and operational for at least a few years, potential investors will surely appreciate the fact that you've already envisioned your company's growth and evolution.

Among other things, your development plan should provide answers to the following questions:

- Is the market for the services you offer currently growing?

- Are you planning to offer line extensions or new services within your first few years of operations?

- Does the market development plan you've crafted offer ways of increasing the overall demand for your services within the industry?

- Are there alternative ways of making your company more competitive?

Remember that the market analysis is a vital part of your business plan and it's likely to take up a large part of the plan itself. This is why it's necessary to conduct a thorough research on the competition and on the market you're planning to enter.

Finally...

You may have the best service in the market, but without an organized and well-crafted market analysis and development plan, you still won't be able to guarantee success. You market analysis helps you identify a clear roadmap of how to bring your services to your target customers.

Financial Projections

Making financial projections for a start-up t-shirt business can be described as both science and art.

Investors may want to see you spell out financial forecasts in cold, hard numbers, but it's not really that easy to predict the financial performance of your t-shirt business several years from now, especially if you're still in the process of raising capital.

Simply put, this is the part where you formally request funding from potential investors and you do that by illustrating how much funding you need for start-up as well as within the first five years of operations.

If you already have an existing business and are looking towards expansion, then you may reflect the funding requirements for the expansion itself.

Potential investors are also sure to appreciate some historical data as regards the financial performance of your company, particularly within the last three years or so, depending on how long you've been in business.

If you have any collateral that can possibly be used to secure a loan, then that's worth noting as well.

Difficulty aside, financial projections are requirements for a solid business plan and you'll really have to deal with them if you truly want to catch your prospective investors' attention.

Regardless of whether your business is a start-up or a growing venture, you'll still need to provide historical and/or projected financial data.

Here are a few useful tips:

1. **Don't let spreadsheets intimidate you**

All financial projections necessarily start with spreadsheet software, with Microsoft Excel being the most commonly used; chances are great you already have the software on your computer.

Other than this, there are also some special software packages that can help you with financial projections. These packages often provide flexibility, which allows you to weigh alternate scenarios or change assumptions quickly whenever necessary.

2. **Create short-term projections as well as medium-term projections**

Specifically, your prospective investors should see financial projections for the first year of operations, broken down into monthly projections.

You should also provide a three-year financial projection that's broken down into yearly projections and a five-year financial projection.

TIP: It's advisable, however, to keep your five-year projection separate from your business plan, but readily available in case a potential investor asks to see it.

When you project business growth, be sure to consider the current state of your market, trends in labour and costs, and the possibility of needing additional funding for future expansion.

3. **Make sure start-up fees are accounted for**

Never forget to include fees for permits, licenses, and equipment in your short-term projections.

You should also keep the difference between variable and fixed costs in mind when making your projections and differentiate between the two wherever necessary.

Variable costs are usually placed under the "costs for goods sold" category.

4. Go beyond your income statement

While your income statement is the basic measuring tool by which projected expenses and revenue can be conveyed, a solid financial projection will go beyond that to include projected balance sheets that show a breakdown of your assets, liabilities, and equity, among other things. You'd also do well to include cash flow projections that reveal cash movement through the company within a given period.

Estimates of the amount you plan on borrowing as well as expected interest payments on those loans should also be included. Furthermore, you should make sure your financial projections are all in accordance to the GAAP.

TIP: If you're new to financial reporting or don't understand the last paragraph, then you may want to consider hiring an accountant to review your projections.

5. Offer two scenarios only

Although you need to go beyond the simple income statement, remember that where financial projections are concerned, potential investors really want to see only two scenarios:

The best- and worst-case scenarios. Anything more than those two are superfluous and may just cause unnecessary confusion, so skip it.

Finally...

To sum up, this section should tell potential investors how much money you need now and in the near future, your preferred type of funding and terms, and how you intend to use the funds.

NOTE: Take note that the intended use of the funds is a vital piece of information for potential investors and would-be creditors, which is why you need to explain it in this section.

It's also important to include all pertinent business-related information that can possibly affect the future financial situation of your company. A trend analysis for your financial statements is also very helpful, especially if you present it with graphs, as this is easier to see.

TIP: Above all, you should strive to make reasonable and clear assumptions.

As previously mentioned, financial forecasting is both a science and an art. You'll need to make several assumptions, but you'll also have to be realistic when making those assumptions. Going overboard will likely raise red flags for potential investors, so always make sure your projections are backed up by solid research.

Calculating Your Start-up Costs

What are start-up costs?

These are the expenses you have to deal with before your new t-shirt business can actually begin operations and earn revenue.

The concept of start-up costs is very important in tax law because these costs are not considered as deductible expenses, unlike most of the other business costs. You will, instead, need to amortize these costs over the course of a few months or years.

This means you'll only be able to deduct part of the start-up costs each year.

And you can only determine and take full deduction on your other expenses after you have determined start-up costs.

The first step

The first step in calculating the start-up costs of your business is to gather all of the expense receipts from business-related transactions.

Next, determine the exact date when your t-shirt business opened and then separate the receipts into two piles: one pile for the expenses from before your business opened and another pile for expenses incurred after the opening day.

You see the reason why many people say it's so much easier to start a home-based t-shirt business than opening one at a retail location is that it requires significantly fewer equipment and materials.

Consequently, a home-based business would entail much less start-up capital as well. In fact, starting a t-shirt business from home can be the perfect test run that can help you determine if it is indeed a wise decision to push through with a full-scale commercial t-shirt business operation.

The good news is that you can get your t-shirt business started with just the most basic business equipment. You may even own most of the needed equipment already.

Once you've decided on the location of your t-shirt business, you can start drawing up the budget for your start-up costs.

Starting a t-shirt business with what you already have on hand is advisable not only because it's cost-effective, but also because it lets you work with equipment and materials you're already familiar with. You could simply add more equipment and materials as your business grows and the need for commercial-grade equipment arises.

The next step is to remove all of the receipts for items such as research costs, taxes, and deductible interest from the pile receipts before opening day. These costs can immediately be deducted.

Finally, add together all the remaining receipts belonging to your "before opening date" pile. The sum is your total start-up costs, which have to be amortized.

Amortization is usually set over a period of 18 months, and expenses like hiring and training costs, pre-opening advertising, and travel expenses to meet potential suppliers are usually included in the amortized start-up costs.

How to Obtain
Small Business Grants

When starting a business there can be some huge barriers standing in your way, among the biggest of which are start-up costs (as discussed) and other business-related expenses.

You may be planning to take out a loan for the purpose of starting your business. Why don't you consider applying for a grant from the government or from private organizations instead?

There are several reasons why grants are better than a loan, the most obvious of which is the fact that grants don't need to be repaid.

How exactly can you obtain a grant and turn your simple idea into a thriving business?

The Catalog of Federal Domestic Assistance is a good place for you to search for a specific grant you can apply for because it contains a list of all grants available for small businesses.

The catalog also indicates what type of business qualifies for a particular grant, so you can immediately determine which grants your t-shirt business is likely to qualify for.

Another option is for you to visit the Small Business Administration's website, which promotes federal grant programs that offer almost $2 billion to small businesses.

Once you have identified the grant programs you'll be applying for, you should start preparing a business plan.

Take note that grant organizations base their approval or rejection of your application on the contents of your business plan.

- Your plan should therefore include a statement of purpose that is clearly written and effectively defines the goals of your company.

- A good business description, an outline of your short-term and long-term goals, a discussion on planned marketing strategies, and a projected financial analysis should also be part of your plan.

The financial section of your plan is very important because organizations usually measure the worth of a candidate based on how you plan to use the grant money.

You should therefore make sure that your financial analysis and hypothetical budget are both conservative and realistic.

When your business plan is complete, it's time to create your actual grant proposal.

If you have previous experience in creating such a proposal, then you can save some money by writing the proposal yourself.

However, if you've never written a grant proposal before, then it would be wise to hire the services of a professional writer.

Make sure your proposal includes schematics, reports, and some basic information on planned projects that are likely to be influenced by the grant funds.

Furthermore, grant reviewers are likely to appreciate such attention to detail, which may be seen as a strong commitment to your product.

In this case, the reviewers will be more likely to approve your applying for grant funds.

Complete your grant application by including an updated list of contacts. This list should start with the contact details of the top-level employees.

It should also include the contact details of individuals who can provide important details on the supplementary materials included in your application.

Make sure that all pertinent information on your business and requested files by the grant organization are included in your application.

If your application lacks any of these files, then the grant is likely to be denied or the processing could be very slow. Submit your application only when you're sure that it's complete.

It's also a good idea to have your grant application reviewed by family, friends, and colleagues so grammatical errors can be cleared up and anything you may have overlooked can be pointed out to you.

And as a final review process, you should schedule a reading session together with your staff, so you can correct any identified problems.

Above all, you should be patient.

Take note that the process of getting approved for grants may take longer to complete than the process of getting approved for loans.

This is because grant applications are reviewed a number of times and most grant organizations have to go through thousands of applications at a time.

Getting Insurance for Your T-Shirt Business

So, you have an idea for a good t-shirt business venture; you even have the name for your new t-shirt business already.

And you've also proceeded to create a business plan and a proposal for a grant application.

What else do you need to do prior to actually operating your t-shirt business?

You will need good insurance.

This is actually one of the most important steps you need to take when starting a business. The good news is that there are lots of places where you can get good advice on the different types of insurance that you may need for your new business.

An insurance agent is probably the best person for you to approach if you're looking for advice on getting insurance for your t-shirt business.

More specifically, you should hire the services of an agent for an insurance company that specializes in clothing business insurance rather than a general insurance company.

You have to understand that you'll be dealing with a totally different set of risks and challenges with a business than you would with insuring a car or with your home.

Getting insurance from a company that specializes in your business sector assures you that the agent you're dealing with really knows what he's talking about.

You can expect the insurance agent to lay out several different insurance options for you.

These options can range from liability insurance for your business to auto insurance. You may also be offered property insurance as well as loss of business coverage, which protects your interests in case a fire breaks out and you end up without a business to run for a month or so.

It's important for you to ask questions and make sure you understand what each type of insurance covers you for so you can be sure to make an informed decision as to which types of insurance you're going to get.

More often than not, you'll be presented with more insurance options than you can afford.

There's also a possibility that the insurance agent you're consulting will present you with more insurance options than your business actually needs. This makes it even more important for you to understand what each type of insurance covers.

Furthermore, the start of a business is usually a time when you will have to take a few risks by taking out less insurance than your business needs.

You'll have to decide how much you can afford to spend for insurance and which type of insurance is the most needed by your business. Once you've determined this, you can leave the other types of insurance for later. Most t-shirt businesses start only with loss of business coverage, others with liability insurance. The point is to get only the most important insurance coverage that you can afford for starters. As your company grows, it will become more important for you to protect your business' assets.

And the good news is that you may able to afford it at that time.

How to Trademark Your Business Name and Logo

If you have just set up a new t-shirt business, you should be careful not to stop at choosing a name and logo for it. You should also make sure that the name and logo you chose is adequately protected.

This is especially important if one of your business goals is to create an instantly recognizable brand.

The best way to protect your business name and logo is to have it trademarked.

Take note that a trademark is also used to protect symbols, drawings, and any other character associated with your t-shirt business, much like a patent protects inventions.

The whole process of getting your business name and logo trademarked is a relatively simple one.

However, it often takes several months for your trademark registration to really become official.

Following is a quick guide on how you can protect your business name and logo by getting it trademarked.

1. Choose the name and design the logo for your new t-shirt business.

   You have to make sure, of course, that the name and logo you choose are not yet being used by any other company.

   More importantly, you need to ensure that such name and logo have not already been trademarked by someone else.

   You can check the database of the official trademark office to make sure you won't run into any legal problems with your chosen name and logo.

2. Once you have established that your chosen business name and logo are not yet trademarked, request for and fill-out the necessary paperwork.

   Once the paperwork has been filled out and submitted to the Patent and Trademark Office, the processing of your application for registration will officially begin.

3. Allow five months for the processing to be completed.

If five months have passed and you still have not received any notification of your trademark having been filed, you may check on its status.

Take note, though, that it usually takes between five and seven months for a trademark registration process to be fully completed.

4. Once you receive notification of your trademark having been filed, obtain a copy of it from the trademark office.

   Take note that you will be asked for your registration number when you make the request for a copy of your trademark certificate.

5. Between the fifth and sixth year of your trademark registration, make sure that an "Affidavit of Use" is filed, so as to prevent other companies from using your trademarked name and logo.

   You should remember to file two other affidavits as well before every 10-year period of owning the trademark has passed.

Writing an LLC Operating Agreement

Limited Liability Corporation, or LLC, is the ideal set-up for start-up companies and small businesses because it requires the business owner to take on only limited liability for the company.

And the good news is that creating an LLC is fairly simple and inexpensive. Take note that the operations of an LLC are governed by the LLC operating agreement.

You'll therefore need to learn how to write your LLC operating agreement.

Here is a step-by-step guide:

1. Gather basic information such as the company name and location as well as the names and physical addresses of the members of your company. You should also note your agent's name.

2. Gather all financial information.

    This includes each member's initial contribution to the company and how much each of them will own in terms of percentage of company interest.

You can choose to have either a single-member or multi-member LLC.

For example, you could choose to initially make a contribution of $100 and own a hundred percent of the company. What's important is for all company members to be included in your LLC operating agreement.

3. Choose and download a sample agreement.

    Of course, you can choose to write your own agreement from scratch, but working from a sample would definitely make the process much easier for you.

    While operating agreements aren't really that complex, the language used can be very governmental, and basing your agreement on a sample will help ensure that the language is interpreted correctly.

4. Determine if you need the services of a registered agent.

    Take note that there's a slight difference in the LLC laws of each state.

The operating agreement typically has a space that needs to be filled in for the registered agent. If your state's requirements allow it, you can be the one to fill in this space.

5. Check the "Business Purpose" section of your sample agreement and make sure it includes the statement that indicates your company's purpose as engaging in lawful acts or activities for which an LLC may be formed.

   You should also check the language in the "Term" section. "Indefinitely" is commonly used for the term.
   In the terms of dissolution, "by a majority" is also commonly used.

6. You should also check the language in the "Management" section.

   A majority of small businesses are managed by the members as a whole, but you also have the option of getting managers for your t-shirt business, especially if there are active and passive members.

Whatever you decide, make sure your agreement contains the appropriate language as to how your company will operate.

7. Personalize the sample agreement by inserting the data from the notes you took as per Step 1 and Step 2. Be sure to include the necessary signature lines.

8. Print the agreement as well as a list of all members with their respective addresses and then staple them together.

   Let all members sign the agreement, have it photocopied, and then provide each member with a copy.

   Be sure to keep the original somewhere safe and have additional copies in your files for reference.

Take note that this step-by-step guide does not constitute legal advice.

If there's anything about forming an LLC that you don't understand, it's still best to seek the advice of an attorney.

Writing a Company Brochure

A company brochure, also known as a corporate brochure, is an excellent way of introducing your t-shirt business to your target market.

That is, of course, if you do it right.

The very first things you need to take into consideration are the logo, font, and color you use on your brochure.

People will only learn about your business if they read the brochure, and they are more likely to read a brochure if the cover has an attractive design, which is why your choice of logo, font, and color is very important.

Take note as well that people are more likely to patronize your business if you're able to build a connection with them and if you're able to establish in their minds the thought that you can be trusted.

The best way to do this using a brochure is to include pertinent information such as the background and history of your company, what you have to offer, and how you intend to deliver whatever it is you're offering.

You may also include information on how your company intends to serve the community as a whole.

Furthermore, you'll need to provide an explanation of what the brochure itself is all about.

- Is it just about the organization or does it present the products and services as well?

- Is it all about the industry and what role your company plays in its development?

- Is it for a specific event where your company is a participant or is it a detailed brochure of your company?

And of course, you'll have to tell the reader at the outset what the brochure's relevance to him is.

Therefore, before you even start writing your company brochure, you'll first have to think about what you want the brochure to portray and who your target audience is.

You may want to set-up a brainstorming session with your company's key personnel for this purpose.

And take note that even as your brochure contains all the necessary information as discussed above, it should remain concise and easy to read.

You should also make it easy for the reader to select which particular piece of information he wants to read. This can be achieved through the use of headings and sub-titles.

As long as you keep these tips in mind, you should be able to create a company brochure that truly presents your t-shirt business in a positive light.

Leasing Space

Having enough space for your business is one of the most critical factors in operating your business so I have included advice on acquiring space in this section.

Among these things are good visibility of the location from the street, and easy access for your customers.

You'll also have to decide if you're going to build, buy, or rent your retail sales space.

There are many advantages to renting space as opposed to buying or building.

Maintenance, flexibility, and taxes are perhaps the three most important advantages.

Maintenance

If you rent retail sales space, you'll be responsible only for a bit of routine maintenance issues like the replacement of light bulbs, repairing uninsured damages caused by negligence on your part, and cleaning the premises.

The good news for you is that major maintenance issues like electrical, plumbing, air conditioning, heating, and structural problems are the responsibility of your landlord.

This means that if your roof starts to leak, it will be your landlord's responsibility to have it repaired.

Knowing that your rent already covers major maintenance issues makes it so much easier for you to budget your company's available funds.

Flexibility

Renting space helps you avoid being forced to stay at the same location even when it's no longer practical to do so.

Even if you have a lease contract for a specific period, that's still a lot better than getting locked into a commercial mortgage.

If the demographics in your area change, then it will be much easier to relocate your business if you're simply leasing or renting space.

This also holds true for the time when your t-shirt business has grown such that you need more space.

Furthermore, you won't have to worry about selling your existing location if you have to move to a new place, which is an issue you'll have to deal with if you own the space.

Taxes

It's very easy to understand the advantages of renting space where taxes are concerned. Rental payments are considered business expenses and are therefore deductible.

On the other hand, only the interest that you pay for commercial mortgages is deductible.

You have to consider as well, the fact that commercial property often doesn't appreciate as much as residential properties, which means your property may accrue very little equity over time.

When you weight this against the 100% deductibility of commercial rent, you'll realize how advantageous it is to simply lease retail space.

Now that you understand the benefits of leasing retail sales space, you'll have to learn how to find the perfect location for your t-shirt business.

Remember that leasing will affect not only your company's profit, but also its ability to grow as well as the satisfaction level of your employees.

So, before you go out looking for space to rent, you'll have to know exactly what you are looking for.

Here's how to identify the perfect retail sales space for your business:

1. Determine how much space your t-shirt business needs now and how much it may need in the future. The rule of thumb in determining space requirements is to have 175-250 sq. ft. of space for each person who will be working at the location.

2. Contact a real estate agent and seek advice in finding a suitable commercial space.

Agents typically have the inside scoop on what'd going on in the real estate market and they can advise you properly on which particular properties are ideal for your purposes.

It's a good idea to contact a real estate firm that specializes in office space rentals.

3. Discuss any necessary improvements with your potential landlord.

    Take note that improvements are usually subject to serious negotiations, especially if there are lots of vacancies.

    You would also do well to check out the parking space.

    Does the rental offer a number of slots you can set aside for yourself and your employees, or would you have to compete with the public for street parking?

4. You may be able to reduce rental cost by either sharing space or looking out for incubators.

You could share your reception area, rest rooms, and conference rooms with another small firm to reduce your rental costs – that is, if you're okay with having less privacy.

Incubators are small unused areas in a larger building which are usually offered for lease at much lower costs.

These are also good options for a small business like yours, provided it meets with your requirements, of course.

5. You may also want to consider renting an all-inclusive suite.

   The rate for executive office suites is usually higher, but they usually come fully-furnished and provide you with access to meeting rooms and office equipment, thus significantly reducing your up-front costs. Many of these suites even come with a receptionist.

6. Before signing a lease contract, be sure to review it exhaustively.

Check the indicated monthly payment, how long the lease is for, what maintenance and repair concerns the landlord will be responsible for, and things like annual rent increases in accordance with inflation.

You'd also do well to check if there are provisions concerning the possibility of terminating the lease early as well as provisions regarding internet connections, cable service, telephone lines, and other company needs.

Other important details for you to review include the date of occupancy, right of refusal for the adjoining space, security, and other amenities.

7. Finally, it's a good idea for you to hire a qualified real estate attorney.

Make sure the attorney specializes in negotiations for leases and that he knows your area.

It's a bonus if he has dealt with the same kind of business in the past.

This is important because lease negotiations typically cover hundreds of terms, which makes it a definite advantage to have someone who's gone through it all before on your side.

Managing Your Employees

Once your t-shirt business becomes successful and grow you may need to employ staff, and you'll have to deal with managing your employees, which can be a very tricky process.

If you're not careful, you just might end up babysitting rather than running a successful business venture.

This is especially true if a majority of your employees are paid very low hourly rates.

You're lucky if you can hire wonderful employees who don't give you any problems.

However, you'll still have to find effective ways of keeping these wonderful employees in your business, and that's where good employee management comes in.

Perhaps the most important aspect of employee management is your ability to set very clear goals and communicate your company objectives very clearly to your employees.

Take note that goal-setting and communicating objectives have to be done regularly.

The more you communicate with your employees in an honest and open manner, the easier it will be for you to manage them.

It's advisable to set monthly, quarterly, and annual goals. And you have to make sure the goals you set are mutual.

This means you should not be forcing your employees to work towards your own goals.

The employees themselves have to believe in those goals and they'll have to be taught how to adjust in case circumstances that keep them from attaining those goals suddenly arise.

Furthermore, you need to realize that goals don't really mean much unless employees' compensations are largely tied up with those goals. The compensation may be in the form of bonuses, commissions, or salary percentages.

What's important is for the employees to have a good motivation for working towards the company's goals.

It's also a good idea to hold a yearly meeting with all of your employees where an annual review will be conducted.

During this review, you should commend your employees for the things they're doing right and discuss solutions for the things that didn't quite work out.

Identifying areas of improvement and finding solutions together can give employees the assurance that they really are part of the company and that they're being valued as individuals, not just as paid workers.

Finally, another very important part of employee management is getting feedback on how YOU are doing at your job.

- How are you as a manager?
- What are you doing right?
- What else can you do to become a better manager?

You have to realize that getting feedback from your employees isn't a waste of your time.

Quite the contrary, in fact.

More often than not, the best ideas for improving a business come from the front-liners, as they're usually the ones who know exactly what the customers want.

How to Market Your T-Shirt Business

Marketing your new t-shirt business probably ranks among the most challenging aspects of putting up a business venture, not to mention that it can also be the most fun. You should, in fact, be excited about marketing your business.

- The main purpose of marketing a business is to let your target customers know that you exist and that you have a lot of benefits to offer them.

And take note that the kind of message you convey to your target market is crucial when you market a new business.

Even if you're selling exactly the same item as your closest competitor, you're more likely to come out on top of the competition if you're able to come up with better marketing strategies and if you can successfully create a brand for your company.

Creating a brand for your company will make your t-shirt business more valuable to potential customers.

In fact, the more you create an attractive personality around your company brand, the more you set yourself apart from the competition, thus giving your t-shirt business a much better opportunity for growth.

How do you know your brand is effective?

Simple.

Market it to yourself.

Imagine that you're a would-be customer taking stock of a new player in the industry.

- Does the company brand look, sound, and feel authentic?

- Is it a fun and attractive brand?

Remember that marketing your business has to be fun, so don't take it too seriously.

And even while you're working hard to create a brand, you should always remain true to yourself.

That is what will make your brand truly authentic.

And an authentic brand is something your competition can never take away.

You Can Do It...

You just have to have the confidence to start and follow a few simple rules.

Treat each customer like a VIP, provide valuable advice and offer exceptional customer service.

Here's a quick recap:

With mainstream fashion sales falling, more and more people are seeking out individual looks and styles from smaller brands. This is definitely the right time for you to enter the clothing scene.

1. Naturally, the first thing you need to do is build on what you already know about fashion and clothing.

    Find experienced business owners who are willing to share their knowledge with you and teach you the ins and outs of the business.

    As much as possible, try to talk to niche designers in a few different towns so you'll get a general idea of what works in a particular neighbourhood and what doesn't.

It's also a good idea to avoid talking to someone working in the same area you plan to cover; remember that you're about to become a competitor. Learn from the mistakes of the other stores you speak with.

2. The next step is to keep track of the latest trends in your locality's clothing market as well as those in your neighbouring towns.

   It's also a good idea to discuss your ideas for the business with someone who's familiar with your area and the fashion industry. Start building a strong network with retailers in the area because they generally know what's hot and what's not in the industry. They can also be your best long-term source of future business. Visit the retailers fashion parties, take them to lunch, and get a feel for what they think will sell.

3. Create a business plan that will serve as your guide and keep you focused even when you have to go through tough times as you start growing your business.

Determine how much you'll need for start-up costs and then discuss how you intend to spend your capital. Determine how much you'll have to spend in marketing your business to consumers, retailers, and third party stores. Aside from guiding you through the process of growing your business, you can also use your business plan to find investors if you feel the need for it.

4. Choose a name for your business and then find out what permits and licenses you need to obtain as well as what taxes you need to pay in order to set up your business.

   It's important to make sure your business is legal to start with because launching any business without securing all the necessary legal documents beforehand can lead to some serious problems later on and may even cause the business to close down.

5. Start marketing your business.

Get business cards made and then start distributing them to potential clients as well as other people who may be able to pass them on to your target clients.

Create brochures as well and then hand them out along with your business cards to other businesses that may be able to help you get clients, e.g. retailers, shoe stores, beauty salons, skateboard shops and tattoo parlours.

When any of these businesses sends you a referral, be sure to send a thank you note. Once you start getting sales, market your business even further by creating a website and then posting information to it.

Advertise your t-shirt venture by distributing flyers containing the name of the business, its location (if you have an office or shop), hours of operation, and your business contact information.

Create publicity and attract customers by holding a mini fashion-makeover show at the local mall or at a nearby venue. You may also distribute flyers and business cards at the show.

Considering designate one room in your house for storage purposes. If there isn't any available space in your home, then you may want to consider renting storage facility or perhaps building a storage shed in your backyard. As your business grows, you may need to rent a warehouse.

6. Set your prices and make sure they cover your business costs, expenses, and payment for your efforts. Do your homework and find out what other t-shirt businesses are charging, and then make sure your prices are competitive. Remember that setting prices too high may drive potential clients away, while setting them too low might give them the wrong impression that your products aren't really that good. You need to learn how to place the right value on your products.

7. Conduct all the necessary research on your target market, on the competition, and on the overall demand for your products in your area before you spend any money on your business venture.

    Among other things, you need to make sure that the location and operational procedures you've chosen are truly what's best for you and your business. Don't just make decisions based on general business rules or on what works for your competitors. Remember that no single strategy will ever work well for everyone, which makes it all the more important for you to find your own best practices.

8. Follow your business plan, but be sure to leave room for adjustments, considering that your market and the overall economic climate can change at any time.

9. Remember that among the most important things you need to ensure when running this type of business is that of remaining competitive.

10. Take out business insurance to cover general liability, product, property, auto, and workers' compensation (when you

employ staff). This will help protect you in case of lawsuits and settlements.

Better safe than sorry.

Balanced business

Finally, you'll need to learn how to balance your business life with your home life. This is where most people encounter problems.

For example, how are you going to deal with having to work on your business on the weekends or late into the evening?

At one point or another, you're going to have to give up some things. It's a good idea to set up a schedule beforehand and let your customers know about this schedule so they're aware of the times when you won't be available.

The above information isn't meant to discourage you from pursuing your dream of running your business. It's simply meant to set the right expectations and prepare you for what might go wrong.

Knowing the things that can possibly go wrong puts you in a better position to take the necessary precautions.

Have fun being your own boss

The great thing about running a t-shirt business is that you get to be your own boss, create your own brand and earn a good income by doing something you naturally enjoy.

Running the business from home will also save you from having to rent an expensive storefront or purchase a commercial building. Of course, that's something you may want to consider as your business grows in the future.

Quality family time

A home business also has the added advantage of providing the perfect venue for you to spend some quality time with your family, as you can bond by helping each other prepare or package your business brochures and advertising paperwork.

In conclusion

When your business is finally up and running, don't be afraid to always try something new. Gather customer feedback and listen to what they have to say.

After all is said and done, you'll surely realise that running your own home staging business can be a truly rewarding experience.

It necessarily involves a lot of hard work, of course, just like any business does. In the end, though, the benefits and advantages you experience will surely be worth it.

All in all, running a t-shirt business may be an excellent way for you to earn a good living while selling great products you love.

Good luck!

8707751R00085

Printed in Great Britain
by Amazon.co.uk, Ltd.,
Marston Gate.